THIS
BIG
SKY

THIS
BY PAT MORA
BIG
PICTURES BY
STEVE JENKINS
SKY

SCHOLASTIC PRESS — NEW YORK

THIS BIG SKY

This sky is big enough
for all my dreams.

Two ravens burst black
from a piñon tree
into the blare
of blazing sun.

I follow their wide ebony flight
over copper hills,
down canyons shimmering gold
autumn leaves.

Two ravens spread their wings, rise
into whispers
of giant pines, over mountains blue
with memories.

This sky is big enough
for all my dreams.

HORNED LIZARD

Still as a rock,
you watch bees, ants,
your wriggly lunch.
I watch you,
carefully put you, bellybulge
pincushion, in my palm,
just for a minute touch
your prickly top.
Puff. A warm balloon
puffs in my hand.

Plop

away you hop across hot sand,
soft, spiny desert creature,
like me.

OLD SNAKE

Old Snake knows.
Sometimes you feel
you just can't breathe
in your own tight skin.
Old *Víbora* says, "Leave
those doubts and hurts
buzzing like flies in your ears.
When you feel your frowns,
like me wriggle free
from *I can't, I can't*.
Leave those gray words
to dry in the sand
and dare to show
your brave self,
your bright true colors."

MOUNTAIN SILHOUETTE

I know an Indian
who never moves.

I watch him sleep
when snow covers
his rock face.

I watch him sleep
when wildflowers burst
open in his eyes.

I watch him sleep
when dreaming snakes
sun on his lips.

I watch him sleep
when wind thumps
its old drum.

I know an Indian
who never moves.

SUSPENSE

Wind chases itself
around our house, flattens
        wild grasses
with one hot breath.
        Clouds boil purple
          and gray, roll
and roil. Scorpions
dart
        under stones. Rabbit eyes peer
from the shelter of mesquite.
        Thorny silence.

My *paisano*, the road runner
        paces, dashes into the rumble,
races from the *plink, plink*
        splatter into his shadow,   leaps
        at the crash   flash
splash,
        sky rivers rushing into arroyos and
thirsty roots of prickly pears,
          greening cactus.

TALL WALKING WOMAN

The sun stares
down with two amber eyes
on the woman, grandchildren
near her knees, who walks tall
to the slow drum beat
of her heart,
a turquoise umbrella above
her head, her blouse, the red
of soft, summer plums,
her skirt, the lavender of rain clouds.

Without turning her head,
the woman watches a teenager
braiding her grandmother's hair
in the shade and young girls
practicing a harvest dance.
Umbrella above her head,
the woman in the plum
red blouse, grandchildren
near her knees, in rain clouds
walks tall through the pueblo,
to a slow drum beat
in her purple tennis shoes.

URBAN RACCOON

Underneath her thick coat she knows—*autumn*,
and she returns to the old tree, her cozy chimney.
She climbs her staircase, gold
and leafy branches, then a strrrrretch onto the roof,
and she ambles along the narrow drain pipe, a swaying,
pudgy tight-rope walker, eyes mysteriously masked.

With a flourish of her ringed tail,
she settles on her favorite spot, rubs her roundness
on the chimney corner, scratch-scratch-scratches
in the warm sunpool with no hurry.
The pudgy lady ignores all horns and sirens.
She just sighs and yawns.

Somewhere underneath her thick coat she knows
wind spins round and around her penthouse, spins
stories all night long about the reddest, sweetest berries
in the world, and she smacks her lips, pours
herself head first into her dark,
safe hole, curls into her furry dreams.

HALLOWEEN

A night of transformations.
Is that dried corn's crackle
or *bruja's* clacking cackle,
the neighbor's dog
or *lobo* lurking in the fog,
and those shadows, stretching closer—
branches of a tree so bare
or bony fingers reaching
for your hair?

Beware.

Tonight, all mirrors lie,
and even candies, sticky chocolate
tricks and treats, may change
and slither
down your throat, quick
flick their slimy tails.

NOCHE

Mountains black
Canyons black
Valleys black
Rivers black
Sky black

Moonless night
Starless night
Windless night
Songless night
Soundless night

Hushed night
Hush

DESERT SNOW

Coyote spies
new moon, slight
grin, high
in the sky.

Coyote licks
cold, white
shine, mouthful
of stars.

Coyote serenades
moon, grinning slyly
at hills sleeping in starry blankets,
at music rising, "Halloooooooooo!"

JOYFUL JABBER

Every morning the jays swoop
into junipers and piñons, bloom
blue on the branches, broadcast
the news that seeds and water
wait on the warm, flat boulder
behind our house.
More than twenty jays gather
at the table, jabber joyful.

I think of my friend far away and wish
we were feasting together,
soaking up this desert light until we too would soar
over cottonwood and aspen tossing
their gold, over cinnamon hills
and the secrets of canyons,
her hand safe in my hand.

ONE BLUE DOOR

To make a poem
listen: crow calls.
Rain paints a door,
blue in the sky.

To make a poem
you need the door
blue and lonely
swinging in the rain.

To make a poem
you need to leap
through that blue door
onto a crow.

To make a poem
you need to glide
on crow's black *caw*,
skimming the trees.

To make a poem
you need to taste
petals of rain.
Open your mouth.

To make a poem
you need to hear
fountains sprouting
in your hands.

Leap through one blue door
onto crow's black call.
Catch rain's petal-fall.
Music in your hands.

Leap through one blue door.

TWILIGHT CHOIR

After the rain,
diamonds scattered
by some careless *duende*
glisten on willow leaves.

Butterflies and hummingbirds
flutter in the breeze.
Poppies fall in moist clusters
where they please,
and stars hum their poetry.

Kittens tease fat cats
dreaming tonguefuls of warm
honey. Trees, dark canopies,
sway melodies.

Their evening song
accompanies cicada whirs
and mockingbird's sassy,
musical originality,
after the rain.

RIVER-MOON

River goes sliding, sliding by.
Río goes gliding under night black sky.
River goes hiding in canyons dry.
Río goes sliding, sliding by.

Moon goes sliding, sliding by.
Luna goes gliding under night black sky.
Moon goes hiding in canyons dry.
Luna goes sliding, sliding by,

river-moon sliding, sliding by,
río and *luna* gliding under night black sky.

GLOSSARY

The words listed in italic in this glossary are Spanish. Words listed that are
not in italic are Spanish, but have become part of the English language.

arroyo	gully	(ah-RROH-yoh)
bruja	witch	(BROO-hah)
duende	elf	(dwEN-deh)
lobo	wolf	(LOH-boh)
luna	moon	(LOO-nah)
noche	night	(NOH-cheh)
paisano	road runner; also, fellow countryman	(pah-ee-SAH-noh)
piñon	pine nut	(pee-NYOHN)
pueblo	village	(PWEH-bloh)
río	river	(REE-oh)
víbora	snake	(VEE-boh-rah)

Special thanks to Roser Salavert, Spanish language consultant.

FOR MY DAUGHTER CISSY WHO LOVES ANIMALS AND DESERTS - P.M.

FOR PAIGE AND ALEC - S.J.

Text copyright © 1998 by Pat Mora • Illustrations copyright © 1998 by Steve Jenkins
All rights reserved. Published by Scholastic Press, a division of Scholastic Inc., *Publishers since 1920*.
SCHOLASTIC and SCHOLASTIC PRESS and associated logos are trademarks and/or registered trademarks of Scholastic Inc.

LIBRARY OF CONGRESS CATALOGING-IN-PUBLICATION DATA
Mora, Pat.
This big sky / by Pat Mora ; illustrations by Steve Jenkins.—1st ed.   p.   cm.
Summary: Poems that describe the landscape, people, and animals of the American Southwest.
ISBN 0-590-37120-7
1. Children's poetry, American. [1. Southwest, New—Poetry. 2. Desert animals—Poetry. 3. American Poetry.]
I. Jenkins, Steve 1952- ill. II. Title.   PS3563.073T48 1998   811'.54—dc21 97-7285
10 9 8 7 6 5 4 3 2 1   8 9/9 0/0 01 02 03

Printed in the U.S.A.   36
     First edition, April 1998
          The illustrations for this book are cut-paper collages.
               The text type was set in Fournier. The display type was set in Trajan.
                    Book design by Marijka Kostiw

```
811        Mora, Pat.
MOR
           This big sky.


$15.95                          YPVE55833
```

DATE			